A Quick Guide On How To Boost Your Credit In 30 Days Or Less.

Sherry Beckley

Dedicated to:

To my loving parents, Larry and Barbara Beckley whose lifetime demonstration of wisdom and knowledge has influence my life. They always encouraged the gifts in their children with godly correction through our Lord Jesus Christ. To my grandparents, Bishop Edward Hackett and Pastor Ann Hackett, who provided the foundation of Jesus Christ in my life.

My children, Diamond and Faith; they give me the motivation to push forward in my life and they always love me unconditionally.

To my brothers Michael and Larry, who taught me to be confident at all times and that life requires resilience. To my sister-in-law Charlotte, who embrace me the day that we meet. To my nephew Tre', who reminds me to put my family first and if one of us succeeds; we all succeed.

To my godmother, Pastor Loretta Douglas; who has encouraged me in every hopeless moment and rejoiced with me in every success. She prayed for me through every stage of life, even when I was less than perfect; she reminded me to always press toward the mark, for the prize of the high calling of God in Christ Jesus (Philippians 3:14).

To the Douglas family, who always embrace me with love.

To my friend Tawnyetta, who all always cheers me up in my lowest moments and who is indeed a true friend at all times.

To all my family and friends who have influenced my life. You have touched my heart in so many ways.

Thank you.

INTRODUCTION

Proverbs 11:14
"Where no counsel is, the people fall, but in the multitude of counsellors, there is safety."

My belief is that every successful person in this world had someone who was a counsellor and no one is really self-made. When you were an infant and did not have the knowledge or the physical ability to take care of yourself, someone had to help you. We all had to learn from someone else and I'm no different; this book was birthed out of hardship, pain, success, failure, wise counsel and my real life experiences. People have helped me along the way and I feel as though I need to help others too. Most of our mistakes in life happen because we were not well informed about a situation, but some of the best taught lessons in life are our failures.

In 2004, I had moved to another state for my job transfer with Ford Motor Company. I was a single mother of two daughters; one was 7 years old and the other was just 8 months. I had previously purchased an investment property in the state I had moved from and now I needed to buy a new house to reside in with my children; I had received a preapproval letter to purchase another investment property.

This was a three family home where I had planned to live in one of the units, when my year lease had expired at the current apartment complex I had rented a few months earlier. I placed the house under contract and the property had been approved by the bank's appraiser. My mortgage broker notified me that in order for me to secure the loan, I needed to increase my credit score.

When I purchased my first home, it was through a FHA loan that only required a 3% down payment. I had to secure a conventional mortgage and I did not have the 20% down payment, so I needed to qualify for a secondary loan for the down for this property. My credit score was at 600, but I never had any late payments on any of my accounts in the past. The closing was in 90 days and I needed to get my score to 660 at the minimum to make the deal work. I had already paid for an appraisal, gave the attorney a deposit and the real estate agency had my earnest money for the contract to be accepted by the seller of the property.

I had invested a lot of money in this process, not to mention, the only way to get my earnest money back from the real estate agency was if the property didn't pass the home inspection. In three months, my credit score was a 680 and I was able to close on my new home.

This situation marked the beginning of my pursuit to really understand how the credit system worked.

Through my years of investing, I have gone through many challenges and have learned that your credit score can be manipulated when you learn about the algorithms that the system is based on.

When you have bad credit, you can gain some of the greatest rewards by just applying some of the simplest techniques in a matter of days. You just need to learn and implement these techniques that can be life changing for you and your family.

Contents

Chapter 1:
Understanding the Banking System.

Proverbs 22:7
The rich ruleth over the poor, and the borrower is a servant to the lender.

To understand how the credit systems work, you must first identify who the bureaus' primary customers are. The answer is the banking institutions. We must look into the banking system process to get a complete understanding. Banks operate under a system called fractional reserve banking. In a fractional reserve system, the bank receives customers' deposits and is only required to retain 10% of the cash. Banks must keep a certain amount of money available for withdraw for their customers in their reserves. The Federal Reserve implements monetary policy for the banking system, by increasing the reserve or decreasing the requirements to control the flow of money into the economy.

The fractional reserve banking method allows banks to lend out 10 times more than their reserves hold in the vault. For example, if you deposit $100 dollars in the bank, they are allowed to lend out $90 dollars and only retain $10 dollars in the reserves. You may have been under the impression that the bank needed your deposits to make loans, but you can see by the illustration of the example that they are guaranteed to make a profit without fully using your money.

How Banks Market Their Products

The credit bureaus are private corporations that offer information to lenders and a give them a list of names of people who they can offer their products. Banks' primary way of making money is by charging interest on loans; they are looking for people who will use credit and will have an ability to pay over a longer period of time to make more money.

Banks' monthly and annual fees are not their primary source of revenue; they are an interest-based system. If the lending institution can charge you a higher interest rate, they increase their profit; this is why the banks and the credit bureaus are so interested in keeping negative information on your credit reports. Bad credit reports are big business and subprime loans are lucrative.

Chapter 2:
The Credit Bureaus.

Proverbs 22:1
A good name is rather to be chosen than great riches, Loving favour
rather than silver and gold.

A person's reputation is very important in this technological age that we have entered. A bad credit score can prevent you from acquiring a job, home and transportation in this country. People are pushed into poverty by their credit reporting history, so it is important to understand who the credit bureaus are and how they work.

Equifax, Experian and TransUnion are the biggest credit reporting agencies in the United States. These credit reporting agencies gather individual credit information then sell the data to creditors and lenders.

How Credit Reporting Agencies Make Money

The credit reporting agencies sale list to credit-card companies, to send pre-approved credit mailings to potential customers. They are also used by potential employers to screen candidates for placement of available job positions as a pre-qualifier. In 2017, Equifax had made more than $3.1 billion in revenue, with a profit of $4.34 billion, while TransUnion had $1.7 billion worth of income.

When you pay your mortgage, utility bills, credit-card payments, auto loans or insurance premiums, these institutions report your payment history through the E-Oscar system to the bureaus. Reported information, purchased information and shared information are used to generate a credit report.

History of the Credit Bureaus

Credit bureaus began back in the 1900s; several bureaus organized as the Associated Credit Bureaus, Inc. Equifax is the oldest of the three major credit bureaus created in the 1900s; TransUnion started around 1968 and Experian was founded in 1980. These credit reporting agencies are the most well-known to the public, but they are not the only major influencers on your credit reporting.

The Two Other Major Credit Information Providers

LexisNexis is a corporation that is a reseller of credit information; they supply your data to credit reporting agencies and insurance companies. LexisNexis Risk Solutions provides the world's largest electronic database for legal and public-records. LexisNexis reports cover numerous aspects of consumers' lives and other companies receive information to determine your insurance renewal, loan approval or job offers.

SageStream LLC, is a company that prepares consumer reports and credit scores for lenders and credit-granting companies. This company provides credit scores directly to lenders who then determine whether to grant or deny you credit or approve you as an applicant. This information influences lenders on your credit worthiness and provides a risk assessment of your current and past information in their database.

The Fair Credit Reporting Act was instated in 1970, because the credit reporting agencies data collection was hidden from consumers. This federal law is enforced by the United States Federal Trade Commission to protect consumers and businesses by limiting the ways in which credit information is reported and shared. The law promotes the accuracy, fairness and privacy of information maintained in the credit bureaus' files. In addition, it gave consumers the right to dispute false information, delete outdated information and remove themselves from unsolicited credit and insurance offers; it further implemented consequences for credit reporting agencies' noncompliance to the law.

These credit reporting agencies are governed by this law and you do have a right to your reports under this act.

Chapter 3:
Understanding How The Credit
Bureaus Work.

Proverbs 4:7
Wisdom is the principal thing; therefore get wisdom: and with all thy getting, get understanding.

The number one problem when it comes to people and their credit is that they just don't understand how the credit system works. If we understand the credit reporting agencies' processes, we would have the battle half-way won. We are now going into a basic overview of the credit bureaus' scoring system.

Each credit bureau has its own unique system, but they generally use the guidelines of a FICO scoring system to generate their credit reports.

How the bureaus measure your credit worthiness.

In 1958, the Fair Isaac Corporation created the FICO score, which is the most widely used credit score. FICO scores range from

300 to 850 and your rating is made up of a three-digit number. There are (5) elements to the score factors as follows:

1. Payment history - 35%

❖ *Have you paid your bills on time in the past?*

2. Balances Carried – 30%

❖ *Outstanding balance Vs Available Credit. (Key Factor)*

3. Length of Credit History – 15%

❖ The longer the credit history, the higher it increases your score.

4. Mix of Accounts – 10%

❖ There should be various types of accounts open.

5. Inquires – 10%

❖ Are you looking for new accounts and not getting approved?

FICO scores can vary due to age, because younger people do not have a lengthy credit history to establish a 850 perfect credit score, which is achieved by only 1% of consumers. A very good credit score is generally 720 or higher. However, people with a credit score below 580 may have problems finding lenders who will extend them credit.

Why the drops in your credit score?

When you begin to continually monitor your credit, you my notice a drop in your credit score. Here are common reasons for lower credit scores:

- ❖ Your payment was more than 30 days late.
- ❖ Amount owed on accounts is too high.
- ❖ Your unpaid account was sent to collections
- ❖ Too few revolving unsecured credit accounts
- ❖ You closed a credit card account
- ❖ Your credit card limit was lowered by the lender
- ❖ Too many request for new lines of credit (inquiries)
- ❖ Too many accounts with balances.
- ❖ Amount owed on revolving credit history is too high.
- ❖ Length of credit history is too short.
- ❖ Too few accounts paid as agreed.
- ❖ Number of accounts with delinquency.

❖ Current past due accounts.

❖ Too few accounts with recent payment information.

❖ Lack of recent instalment loan information.

❖ Credit cards over maximum limit.

❖ Proportion of balances to credit limits is too high on revolving accounts.

❖ Negative Public records (Tax liens, bankruptcy, foreclosure)

How do the credit bureaus identify each consumer?

The credit reporting agencies create a database credit file for each consumer. They use (10) basic identifiers as follows:

❖ Social Security Number

❖ Date of Birth

❖ First Name

❖ Last Name

❖ Numeric Address

❖ Street Name

❖ Zip Code

❖ Middle Initial

❖ Previous Address

❖ Spouse

It is very important to review your credit report and remove any incorrect name spellings, out date or unfamiliar addresses from you credit file. Inaccurate information may cause your credit file to merge with another person's credit history and cause incorrect reporting on your credit score.

Chapter 4:
How To Analyze Your Credit Score.

Proverbs 20:4
(Contemporary English Version)
If you are too lazy to plow, don't expect a harvest.

When you begin this journey of working on your credit, it's going to require you to invest your time and money in your efforts. You must be willing to commit to changing the habits that got you in this financial situation.

You must have constant access to your credit scores, so I strongly advise you to invest in a monthly monitoring credit subscription that will give you access to all (3) credit reporting agencies; Equifax, Experian and TransUnion. Use a free subscription such as Credit Karma as a starting point to see what information is reporting on your Equifax and TransUnion score, but it will not give you the most accurate information. You should also order all your credit reports by certified mail, because these monitoring reports may have missing information that is actually on your hard copy reports; here are the addresses below:

Equifax
P.O. Box 740256
Atlanta, GA, 30374

TransUnion
P.O. Box 2000,
Chester, PA 19022-2000

Experian
P.O. Box 2104
Allen, TX 75013

Scoring and Factors

Payment History

This category will make up an approximate 192.5 of your scoring points. You need to look at past due balances, especially any past due payments over 30 days old. Late payments in the last three months can drop your credit score by 50 points. You will need to bring these items current as quickly as possible.

Collections and charge-off accounts can cause your credit score to decrease by 50 points in the first month when these items. The older the collection become, the more the effects should minimize, but your score can remain 23 points lower than its original starting point.

Public Records is another factor such as bankruptcy, foreclosure, judgements and tax liens. These items can impact your score by up to 100 points in the first month when they initially report. The effect of these items will minimize as time passes.

Amounts Owed

When you have too many accounts with balances that are high than your available unsecured credits such as revolving credit card accounts: This can adversely affect your credit score in a negative way. Your debt to available credit ratio accounts for an approximate 165 points of your score.

New Credit

Too many recent credit inquirers can negatively affect your score. Each new credit hard pull can deduct 5 points off your credit score. Too much new credit can also hurt your overall score. The banks will see as a person who is desperate because you are not financially stable and need immediate funding. You should not have more than 3 inquiries within a 12 month period. Studies have shown that people with six or hard inquiries on their report are more likely to default on their loans. This scoring category comprises of an approximate 82.5 points of your credit score.

Credit Mix

Not having a variety of trade line accounts can hurt your credit score. Lenders like to if you are financially responsible to manage different types of accounts. An unbalanced credit mix can be a negative indicator to lenders. This is an approximate 55 points of your credit score.

Length of Credit History

If you do not have credit aged accounts, then your credit report will have a lack of sufficient credit history. Since lenders make money off interest, they want to see your ability to pay your accounts over a longer period of time to determine your credit worthiness. Look at the age of your oldest accounts, because this comprises of an approximate 55 points of your credit score.

Keep A Credit Journal

Write down your problematic areas of your credit profile. Make sure you start with the items that are in the higher scoring category as you list those items. Document the date of the reporting, names of the companies, the business address and the phone numbers. Look for items that are inaccurate and incorrect in their reporting.

Compare the information on all three credit reports and document any inconsistencies in the reporting. If there are any aliases, misspellings of your name, old and unfamiliar addresses, you will need to correct these items with the credit bureaus through the dispute process. In addition, make sure you keep track of the date that you mailed your correspondences so you can be as efficient as possible with responses from the credit bureaus.

When you are contacting the creditors or collection agencies directly, make sure you keep the time, date, first and last name of the person you spoke to in reference to your issues. If they refuse to give a name, you can look up the Better business bureau website and they will have names of the broad members or contact person in that company that you can address your letters to via US certified mail. Remember not to sign these correspondences, so your signature is not copied and pasted to any documentation.

Chapter 5:
Strategies To Increase Your Credit In 30 days or less.

Proverbs 12:24(NET Bible)
The diligent person will rule, but the slothful will become a slave.

The Merriam-Webster dictionary's definition of diligent is characterized by steady, earnest and energetic painstaking effort: If you want to increase your credit, you must be diligent to manage your credit or you will be a slave to a lender working to repay their loans.

If you want to raise your credit fast, you must look at your starting point of your credit score to understand the strategy you must take. A person starting with a low credit score below 600 will see more of an improvement on their credit score with simple changes than someone who is already at a 700 credit score. When you are at a different starting point, you need a different approach.

To make these strategies work, you must be current on your payments on open credit accounts; this does not include collections, but if you have had any negative information added to your credit in the last three months, understand the greatest drop in your credit score will be in that time period. Make sure you have all your accounts current so you can see the greatest results when you apply these techniques.

Understanding Debt to Credit Ratio- The Key To Success

When people try to work on their credit, they begin to try and remove negative items first; they should first start with their debt to credit ratio. The most fraudulent belief is that you have great credit because you don't have a credit card and you pay all your bills in full every month. This false belief totally goes against the credit system. As I mentioned in previous chapters, banks and lenders make the most of their money when you are carrying a balance over a longer period of time and pay them interest.

Your debt to credit ratio is your debt to total available credit and it should be no more than 30% on your credit report. For example, if you have a $5,000 unsecured credit account and are in debt $1,500, then your debt to credit ratio is 30%. Your true credit worthiness is shown by your ability to maintain balances and pay over time. If you carry the correct debt to credit ratio, you can immediately boost your score faster than removing negative items, by adding unsecured revolving credit accounts.

No Unsecured Revolving Cards

Your credit score is driven by unsecured revolving credit such as credit cards. You may have had a credit card cancelled, closed or credit line reduced in the past and saw an immediate drop in your credit score; the credit system is designed to make money off you; not for your personal benefit. Banks will only extend unsecured revolving credit to you only if another bank has currently given you a credit limit; and they will usually only match the line of credit you currently have. For example, if you have a credit card from ABC Bank with a credit limit of $2000, then the next credit card company will match that limit at $2000 too. What do you do if you have no credit cards or want to increase your credit line to increase your credit score?

Merchandise Cards

In my book *A Quick Guide How to Boost Your Credit Fast with Merchandise Cards*; I go into detail on how merchandise cards are the key to balance the debt to credit ratio problem or no credit situation.

If a person has no credit cards, you can get a credit line for a membership fee, most times, with no credit check and guaranteed approval. This revolving unsecured line of credit is for their online store only; but they will report the line of credit to one or more credit bureaus. You will be able to get credit card offers from banks so you can obtain a bank credit card. A person with no credit will benefit in the areas below:

Payment History	35%	X
Balances Carried	30%	X
Age of Credit	15%	
Mix of Credit	10%	X
Inquiries	10%	

A person with a thin credit file can establish on time payment history, offsite any debts that they have reporting on their credit and add a variety of credit to their credit file. You can see a 50 point increase depending on your credit score.

High Revolving Credit Card Balances

You are like most Americans and your credit card balances are higher, but you don't have the money to pay your balances off; merchandise cards can be a cost-effective option to decrease your debt to credit ratio. For example, if your credit card line of credit is $10,000 and you owe $8,000, then your debt to credit ratio is 80%. By adding a merchandise card with an unsecured revolving credit limit of $5,000, you can reduce your debt to credit ratio to 30% for less than paying down the credit card and increase your credit score. Here are the benefits below:

Payment History	35%	
Balances Carried	30%	X
Age of Credit	15%	
Mix of Credit	10%	X
Inquiries	10%	

Merchandise cards can transform your credit score virtually overnight if you know what to look for in the requirements. I go more in-depth in my book: A Quick Guide How to Boost Your Credit Fast with Merchandise Cards if you need more information.

Paying Down Current Card Debt

Sometimes, the best options are the simplest ones; if you have small limit store card cards and they are at or over the card limit, you need to pay them down below 30% utilization rate. You can increase your credit score in a day if you call you credit card company and ask them on what date they report your credit card to the credit bureaus; and pay down your card before that date.

If you have a number of credit cards and find out each one's reporting date, instead of paying all your cards at once, you can use your resources most effectively or pay $25 dollars every week out of your pay check on the card. This will reflect an increase in your credit score. Here is the benefit as follows:

Payment History	35%	X
Balances Carried	30%	X
Age of Credit	15%	
Mix of Credit	10%	
Inquiries	10%	

It is very easy to max out smaller credit cards, so by managing these cards' balances, you can see a 26 point increase in your credit score overnight.

Authorize User Accounts

It is possible to use another person's good credit history and merge it with your own credit. You can piggy back off someone else's credit card payment history to help offset negative payment and add age and length of history to your credit report. If you have a parent with good payment history on the credit card account, you can be added as an authorized user. They do not need to give you the credit card with your name on the card, but they can hold it for safekeeping.

The drawback to this method is, if the person's debt to credit ratio is high or they miss a credit card payment, this will immediately hurt your credit score. This is still a highly effective way to increase your credit score in 30 days. Here are the benefits:

Payment History	35%	X
Balances Carried	30%	X
Age of Credit	15%	X
Mix of Credit	10%	X
Inquiries	10%	

Collections on Your Credit Report

Collects can be a very frustrating situation to deal with when it comes to your credit. Third party collection companies buy your debt from the original creditor for as little as ten cent on a dollar to make huge profits. When the original creditor charges off the account, they receive a tax credit from the IRS so they can no longer collect the debt from you personally; or they will now make a profit from the IRS tax break and your payment.

For example, if you owed a card credit company $500 dollars and then they charge it off on their taxes; then in return, you pay them the $500 dollars. Then they really made $1000 dollars in profit. The IRS will consider this as an unjust enrichment and they can face penalties, so in return, they sell the debt to the collection company to make more profit off already charged off debts.

The Law of Contracts

A contract is an agreement that a party can turn to a court to enforce; to have a valid contract, both parties must intend to be bound by the contract. The problem with credit card accounts especially, people rarely sign the contract and send it back to the card company; they simply use the card. The catch is that you never agreed that the credit card account can be sold to another company so the card company has no legally write to sell that debt without your consent.

Collections agencies are aware of the fact that they have no written agreement to collect so that is why they record your phone conversation; when you agree to pay them over the phone you make a verbal agreement. If you tell them you do not want your phone call recorded they immediately disconnect the call. You should always be carefully when you speak to this agents of the phone became you can make their debt legal by saying the wrong things.

Debt Validation

Debt validation is your federal right under Fair Debt Collection Practices Act. You have a right to request a debt validation, you must send a written request to the debt collector within 30 days of initial communication. If the debt collector don't respond within 30 days they must stop attempts to collect the debt including:

- ❖ Reporting on your credit report.
- ❖ Phone calls
- ❖ Written letters

You can send a validation letter after the 30 day validation period but they are not legally required to respond to your request after that timeframe. The important part to this process for you is that the collection company is not permitted to list the item on your credit report while it is in the 30 day validation period and a collection can decrease your credit score up to 50 points. Here are your benefits as followed:

Payment History	35%	X
Balances Carried	30%	X
Age of Credit	15%	
Mix of Credit	10%	
Inquiries	10%	

Collection can easy removed from your credit report with a few credit strategies. ***My book a Quick guide how to boost your credit and stop collection;*** goes in depth with techniques to remove collection accounts.

Student Loan debt

44 million Americans collectively have borrowed $1.5 Trillion dollars in student loan debt; if you are one of those people like I was, you know that is a very costly bill to handle. Student loan missed payments can destroy your credit history and you can eventually default on your loans. If you are struggling with your student loan payment and do not want to have late payments on your credit report, there are two options that may help you and you can have processed within 30 days.

Loan Deferment

Student loan deferment is generally the better option if you have subsidized federal student loans or Perkins loan; if you have a hardship such as unemployment, health issues or dealing with a significant financial situation this maybe your best choice; because interest does not accrue on subsidized federal student loans and Perkins loans, but you may need to make certain criteria to qualify for approval.

Forbearance

Student loan forbearance is the next option if you don't qualify for deferment and your financial challenge is not a long term situation. Usually, you are not allowed to receive forbearance for more than 12 months and interest will be accrued on the loans.

The plus side to both of these options is that you will not have your credit impacted over late payment and this will prevent the loans from defaulting. Here are the benefits for your credit:

Through my years of investing, I have gone through many challenges and have learned that your credit score can be manipulated when you learn about the algorithms that the system is based on.

Payment History	35%	X
Balances Carried	30%	
Age of Credit	15%	X
Mix of Credit	10%	X
Inquiries	10%	

Neither of these two options are a good long-term solution but it can keep your credit score from being damaged. If you are in default I discus some options in my book A quick guide how to get student loan relief and improve your credit score.

Inquiries

Inquiries can cause great damage to your credit report; each hard pull inquiry can reduce your credit by five points. It is important to look at a few factors when you are looking at inquiries:

❖ The age of the inquiries

The inquiry are only allowed to report on your credit report for 24 months You should dispute through the credit bureaus to remove any inquiry that is over 24 months in age.

❖ Authorization

You must give a company your authorization in order for them to access your credit report. If a company did not receive your written consent via an application or contract you can demand that the inquiry be report from reporting on your credit report.

If they don't provided proof you can filed a lawsuit in your local small claims court for defamation. The actions of this company is causing a financial loss by defaming your character to other lenders. Make sure to call the company and obtain two employees names to include in the lawsuit. You should try to make the less than $600 dollars so will be in the companies' best interest to settle the case than to hire an attorney to fight the lawsuit.

Removing inquiries can improve these areas of your credit below:

Payment History	35%	
Balances Carried	30%	
Age of Credit	15%	
Mix of Credit	10%	
Inquiries	10%	X

Remember to always sent letters via certified mail and do not place your signature on the letters so these companies will not be able to copy your signature and add them to documents.

In conclusion these are some strategies that will help you increase your credit score in 30 days or less; when you apply these techniques for 6 months you may see an 150 point increase in your credit report. Have many more in depth techniques included in my other book titles to help with various credit problems.

Inquiry Deletion Letter

Your Name

Address

City, State, Zip Code

Company Name

Address

City, State, Zip Code

Date

Legal Department,

This letter is to notify the management named as (EMPLOYEE NAME) that your company placed and unauthorized inquiry on my credit report on 00/00/0000.

I demand under FCRA: Section 604:

1. **Permissible Purpose**
2. **My written authorization**
3. **Proof that I personally initiated this inquiry.**

Either provide me strict proof or **DELETE** the item immediately. If you do not delete the inquiry in 15 days I will take legal action.

Under 15 USC Section 623 you have 30 days to do a reasonable inquiry into this matter. If you ignore this letter and do not delete the inquiry or don't provide STRICT proof of authorization I will have no other choice but to have my local Congressman promptly forward a formal complaint to the Federal Trade Commission and Attorney General for further scrutiny of this matter. Your cooperation in advance is appreciated.

Sincerely,
YOUR NAME
U.S. Postal Certified Mail Number: XXXXXXXXXXXX

www.ingramcontent.com/pod-product-compliance
Lightning Source LLC
Chambersburg PA
CBHW030543220526
45463CB00007B/2958